Copyright

Copyright ©2021 by Color Me Black All Rights Reserved.

No part of this publication may be reproduced, distributed, or transmitted in any form or by any means, including photocopying, recording, or other electronic or mechanical methods, without the prior written permission of the publisher except in the case of brief quotations embodied in reviews and certain other non-commerical uses permitted by copyright law.

Conceptualization by Shyle Woods
Illustrations by: Shayla Williams of Shay Design Studio

For more information, visit us online at
http://Colormeblack.shop

Note To The Community

When your mind often wanders, let it. Sometimes that's our sign that we need a mental break from the reality in which we live.

Explore the creativity in which your mind often tries to challenge you with. You would be surprised what can come forth when you just let your mind wander and explore.

Now let us create something beautiful.

                Much Love, Color Me Black

The Power in Words

Find the words listed below.

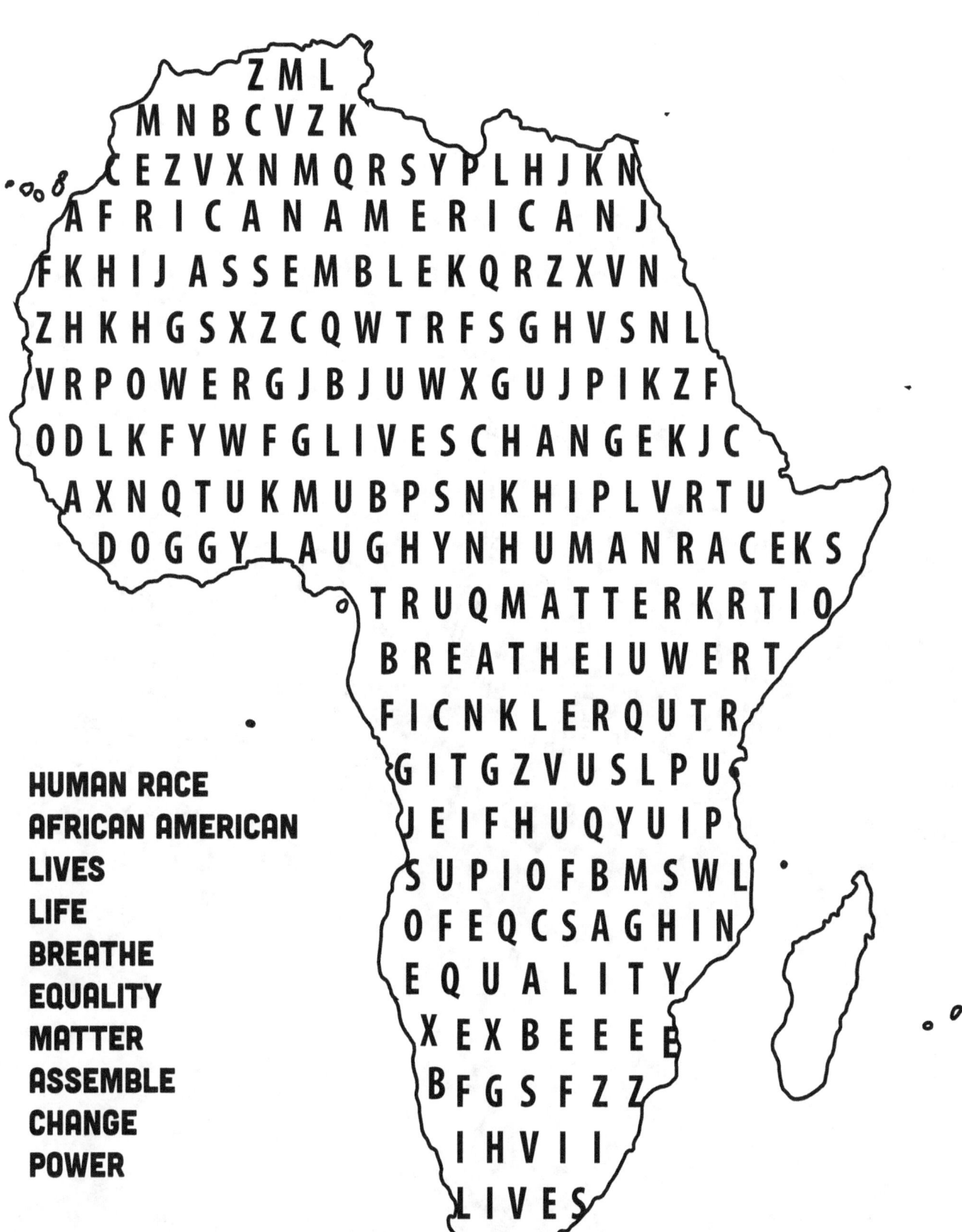

HUMAN RACE
AFRICAN AMERICAN
LIVES
LIFE
BREATHE
EQUALITY
MATTER
ASSEMBLE
CHANGE
POWER

Connect The Dots

Connect the dots and find out just how valuable you are!

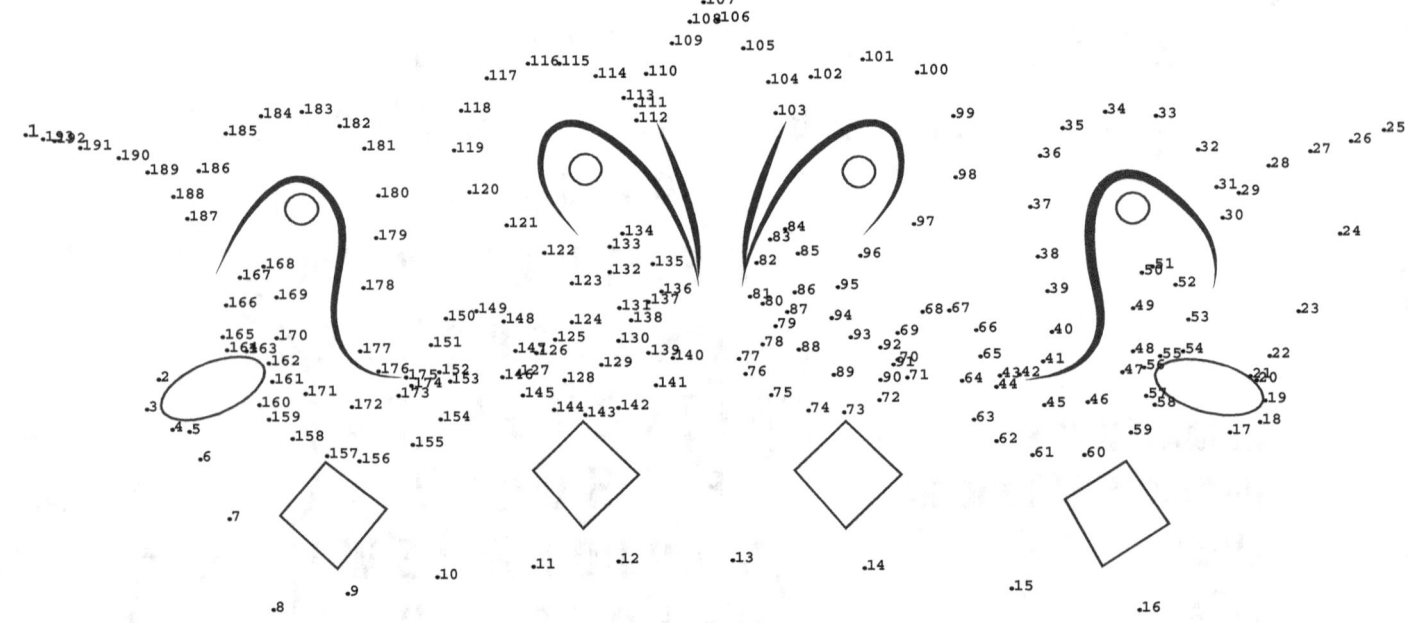

Maze Escape
Help Kiana find her crown.

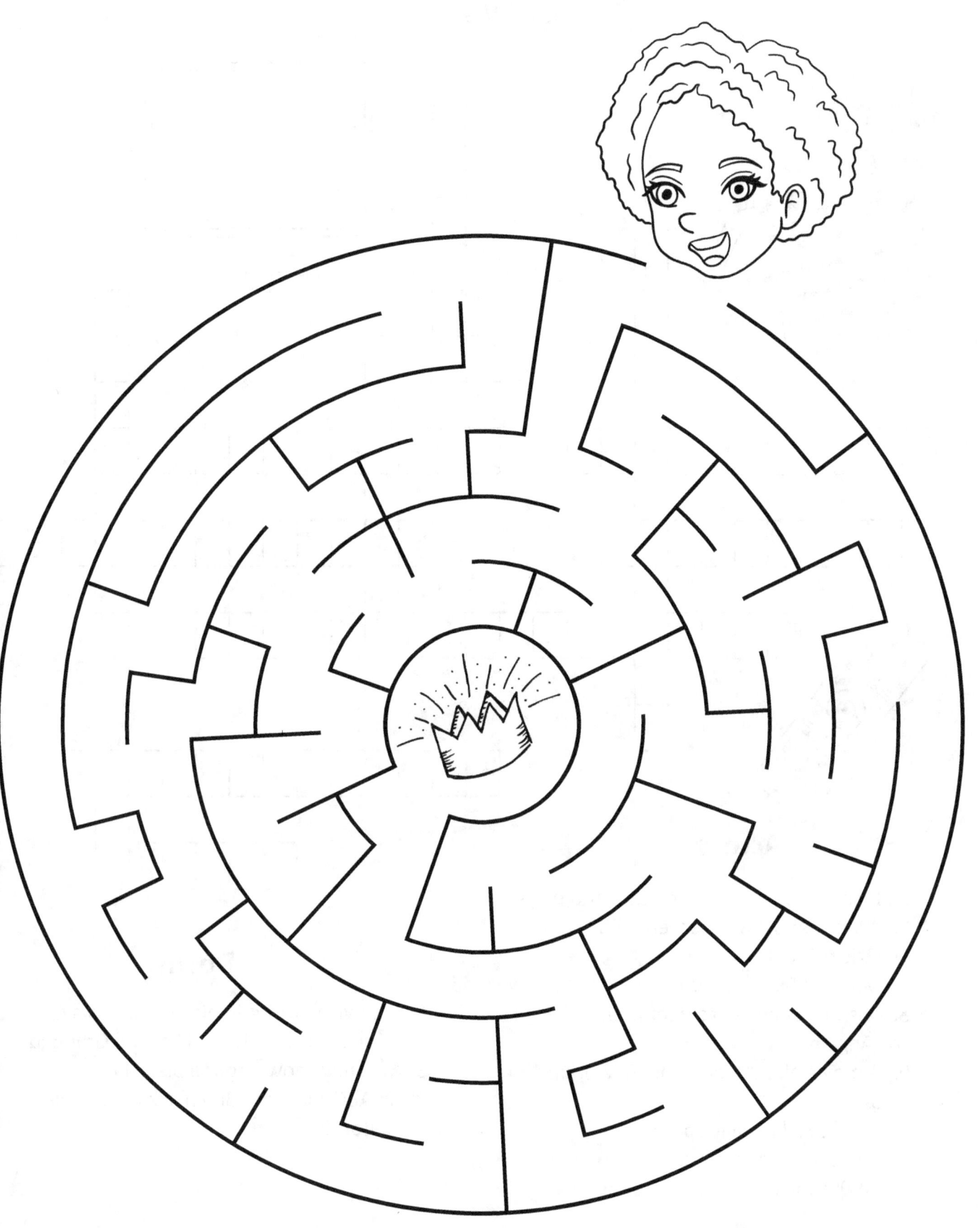

Black TV shows and Movies

Fill in the crossword with the names of these popular black movies and TV shows.

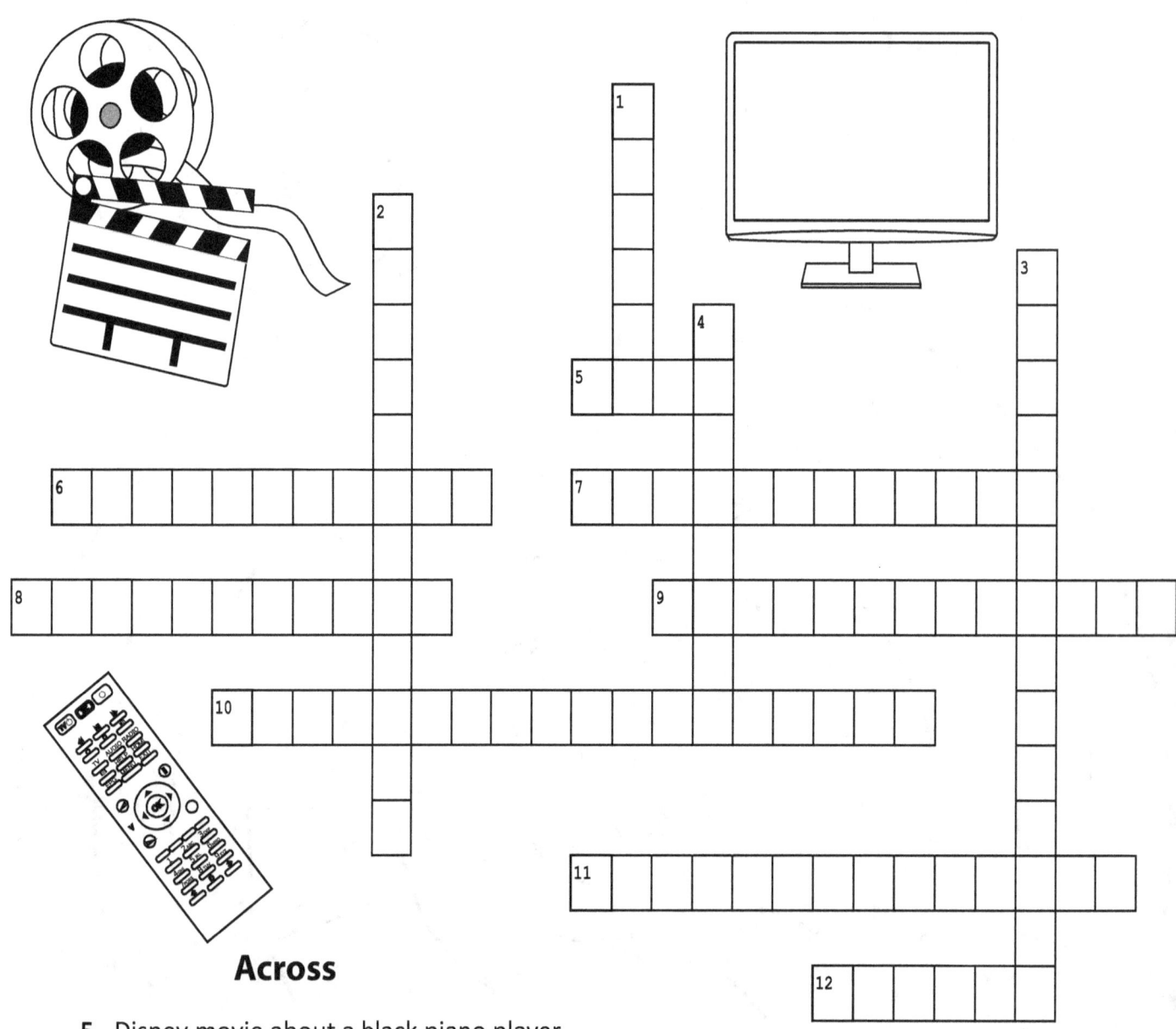

Across

5. Disney movie about a black piano player
6. A show about a superhero with electric powers
7. Marvel's Black Superhero who lives in Wakanda
8. TV show about a group of friends living in Los Angeles
9. A movie about black women working for NASA
10. Disney's first black princess
11. A TV show about a superhero family
12. A 90s movie starring Ice Cube

Down

1. A movie starring Jamie Foxx as a slave
2. TV show about Huey, Riley and Grandad
3. A Disney show about a black family
4. An ABC show about a black family living in California

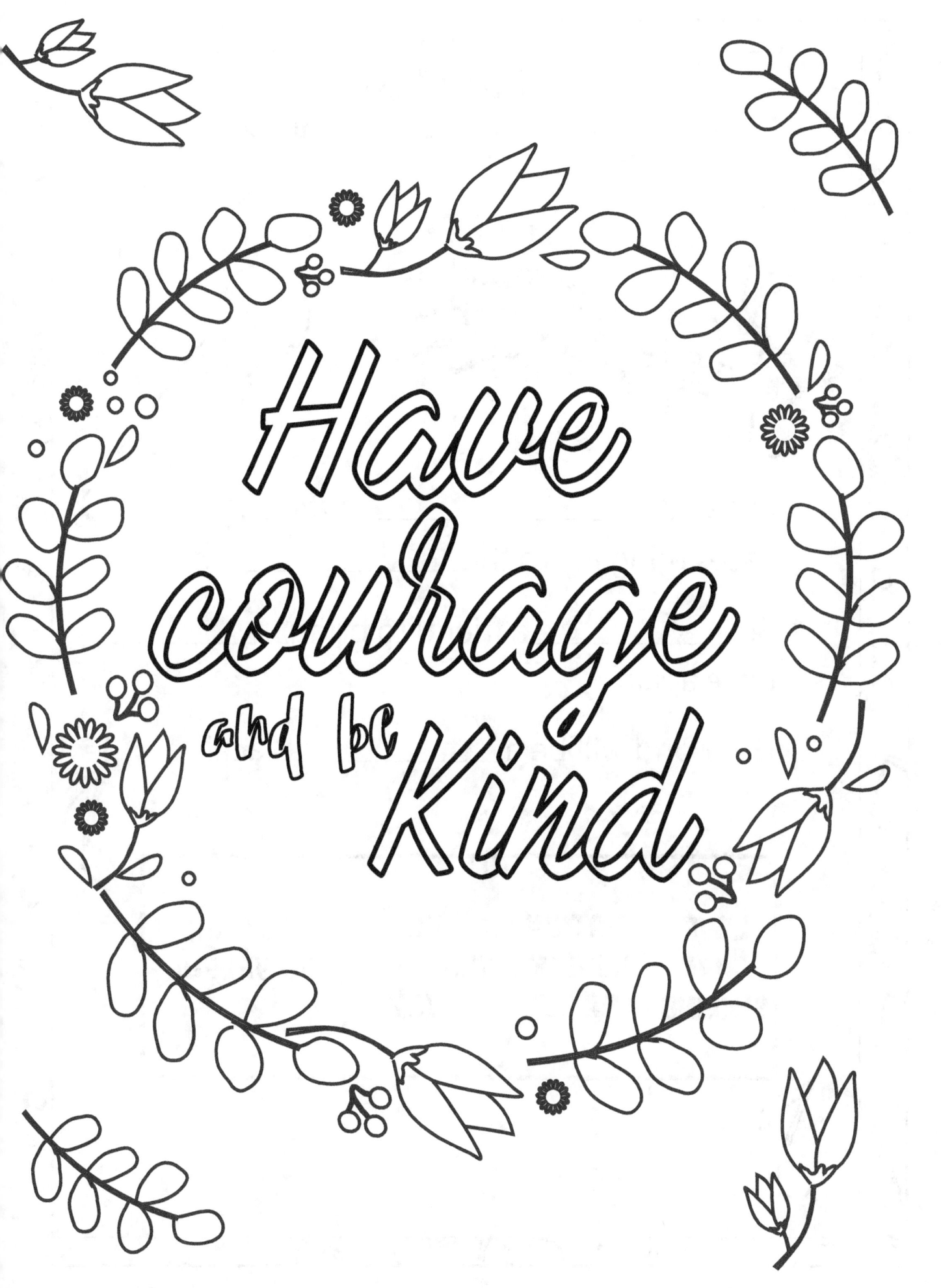

Sing That

Fill in the blanks with words to finish the poem.

Put a little _____ in the air!

Faces bring joy to the _____ .

So _____ a friend to bring _____ once again.

The world will be a _____ place!

LOVE	NATION	HUG	BETTER
CARE	GRINNING	HIGH-FIVE	POWERFUL
SMILING	RACES	JOY	

Power To The People Word Search

Find the words listed below.

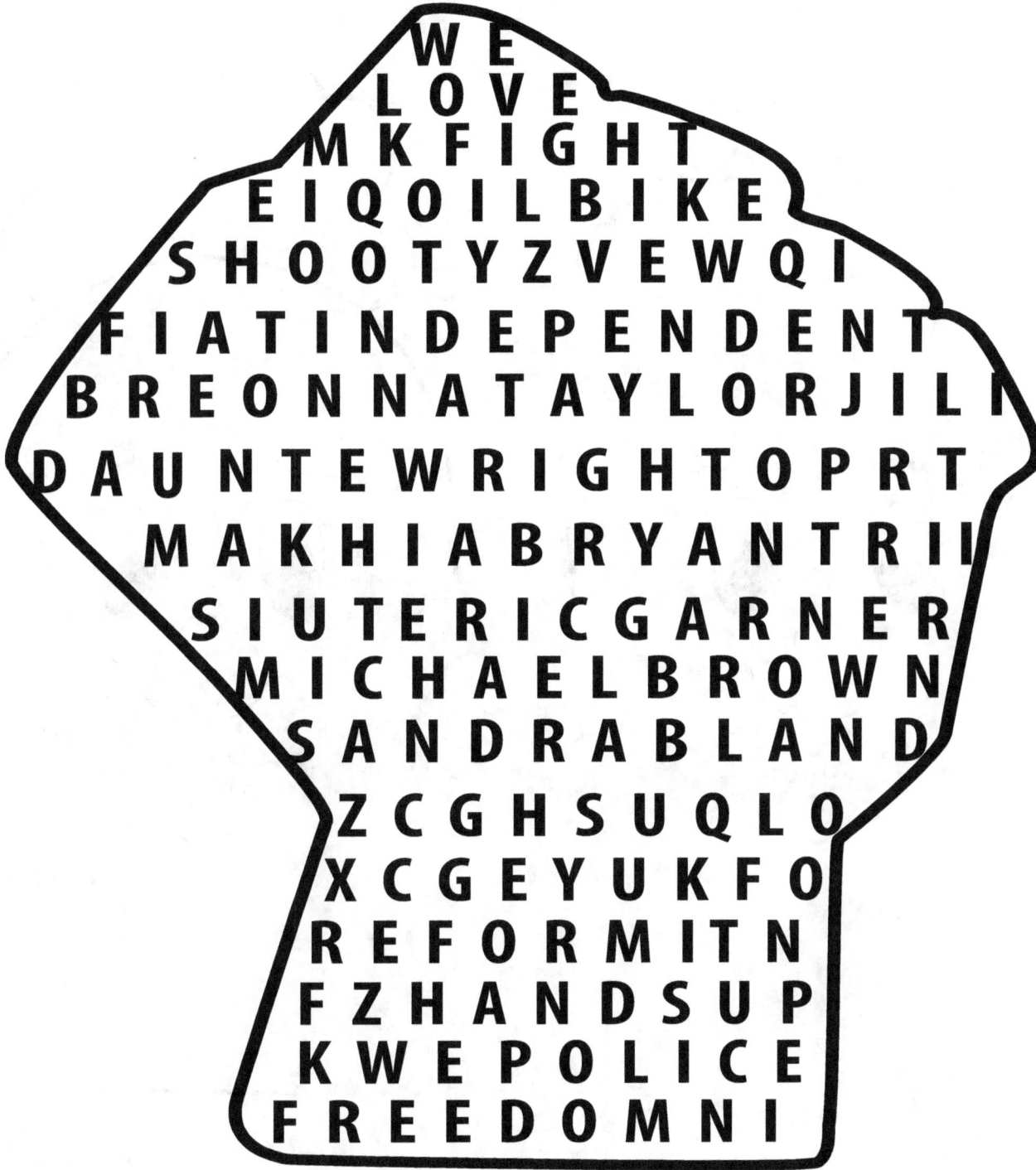

HANDS UP
SHOOT
POLICE
FREEDOM

MAKHIA BRYANT
DAUNTE WRIGHT
INDEPENDENT
ERIC GARNER

REFORM
SANDRA BLAND
BREONNA TAYLOR
MICHAEL BROWN

Connect The Dots
Complete the drawing by connecting the dots.

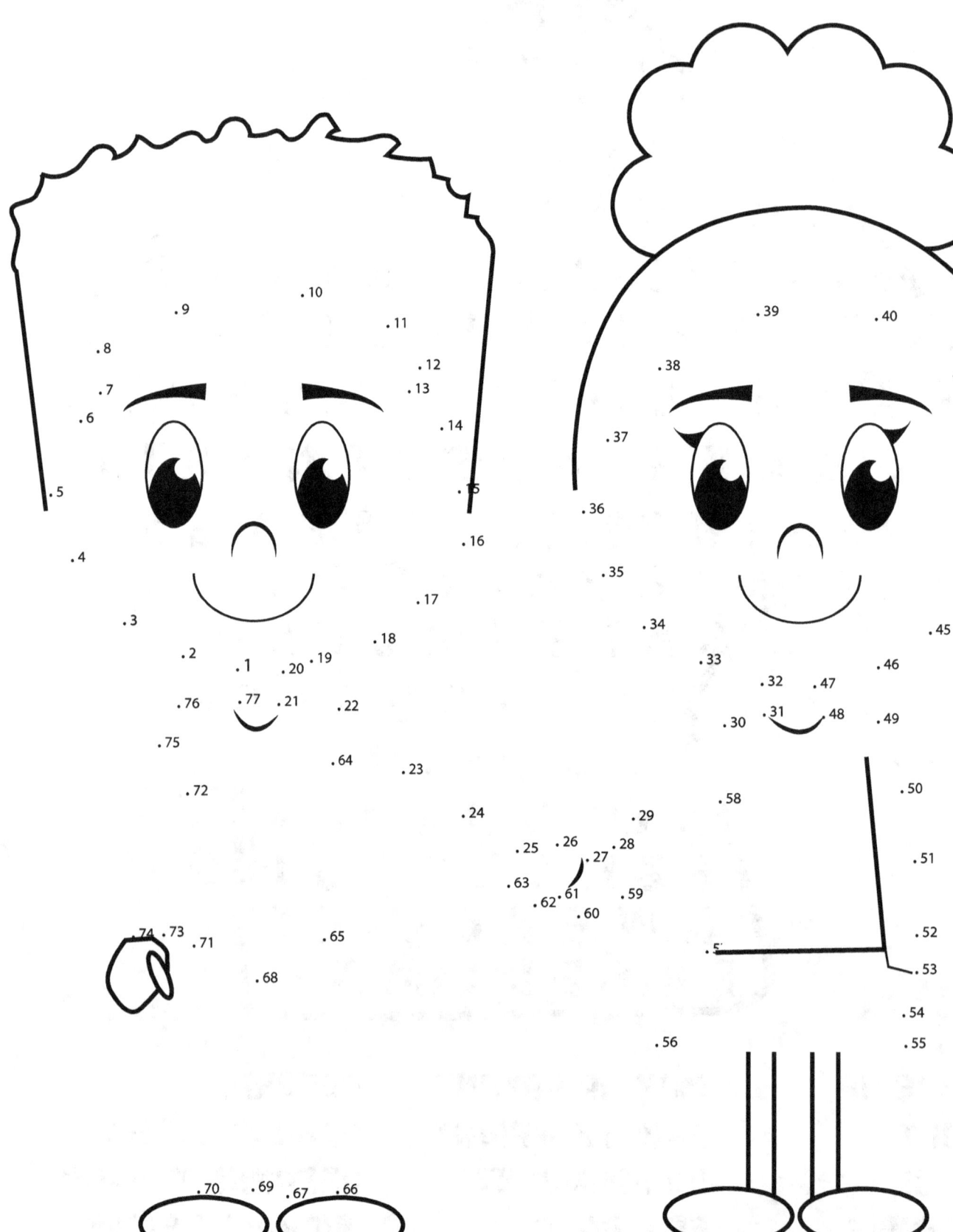

Maze Escape

Help Kyrie find the nearest Black Lives Matter protest.

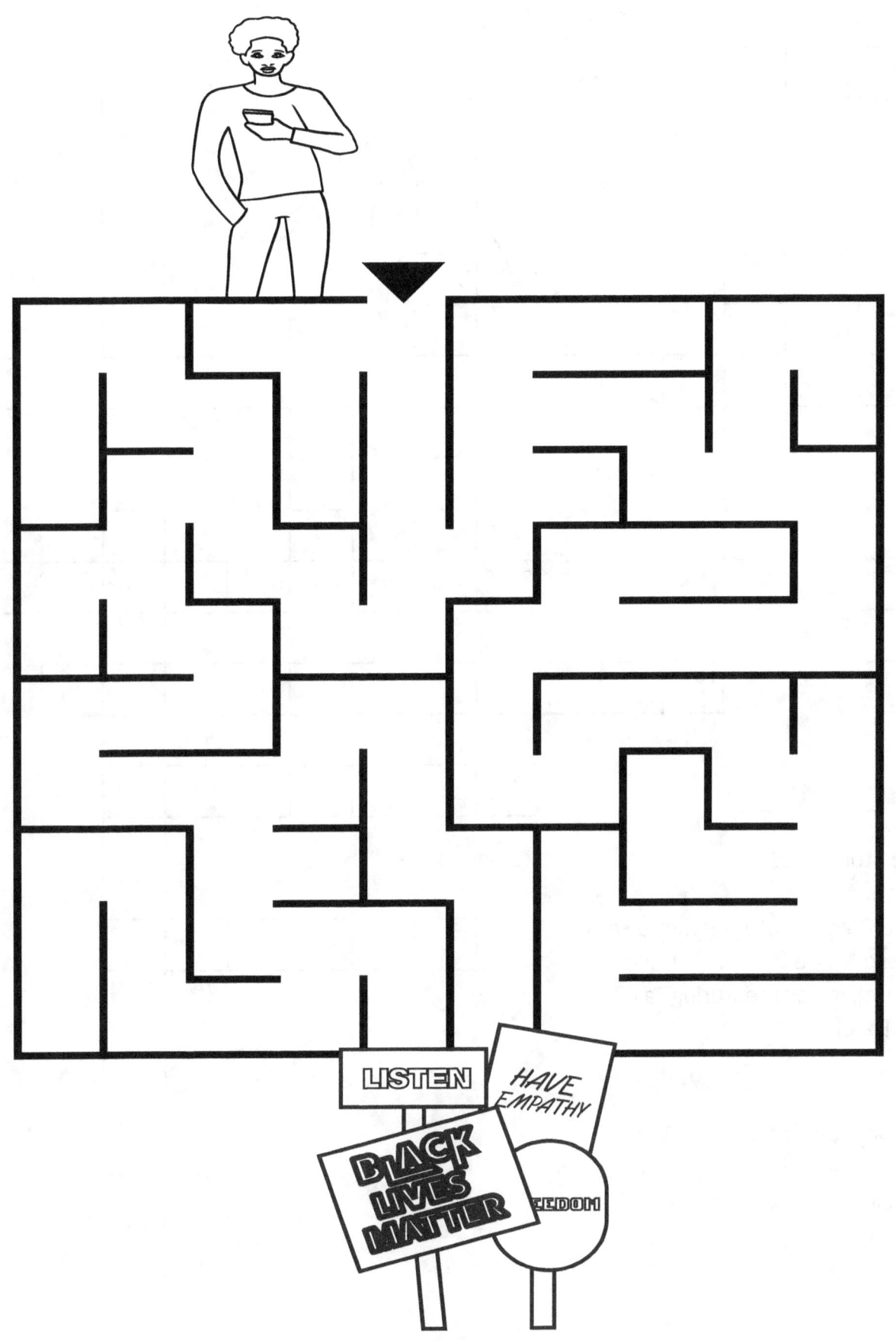

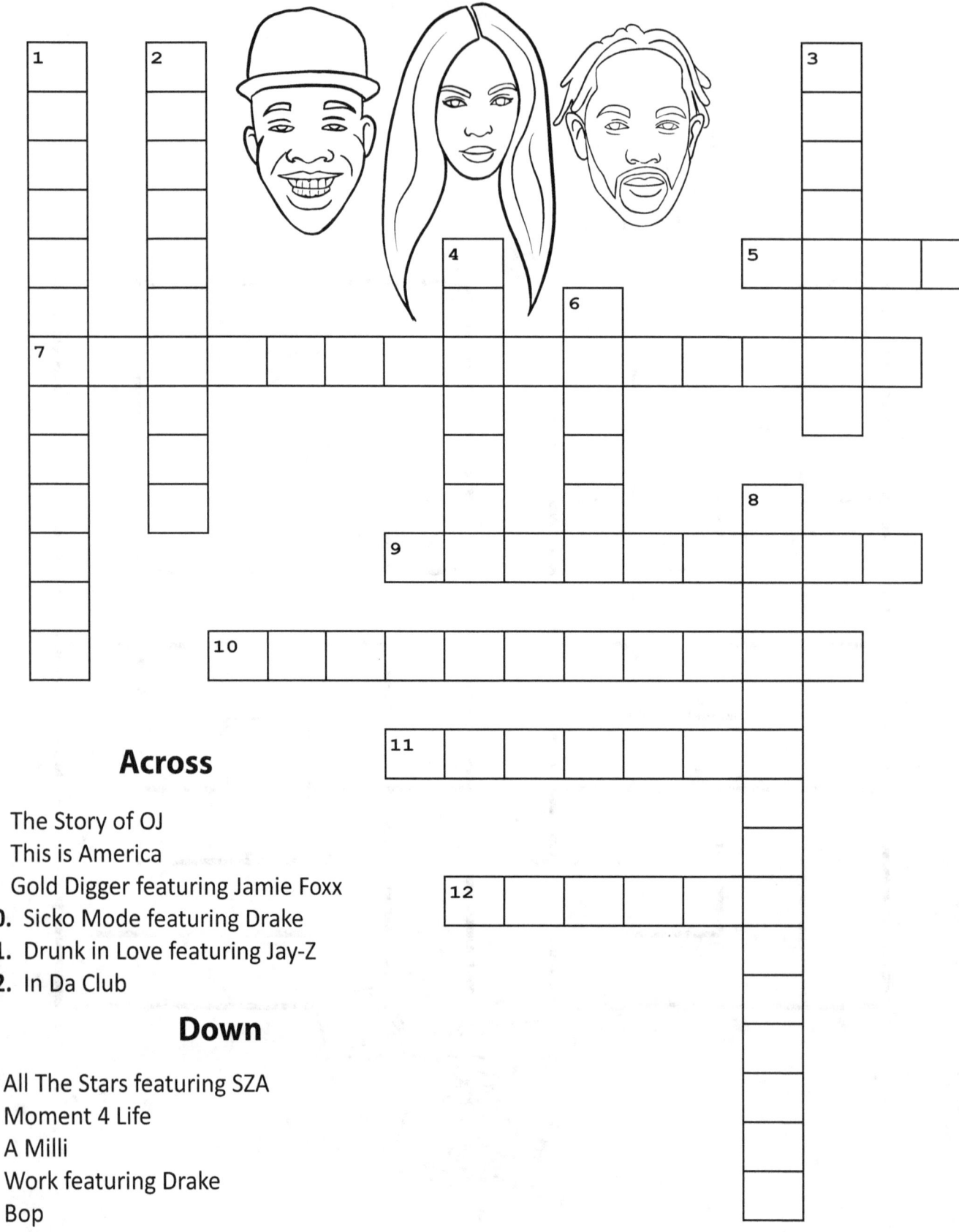

Black Artists and Music

Fill in the crossword by matching the artists with their songs

Across

5. The Story of OJ
7. This is America
9. Gold Digger featuring Jamie Foxx
10. Sicko Mode featuring Drake
11. Drunk in Love featuring Jay-Z
12. In Da Club

Down

1. All The Stars featuring SZA
2. Moment 4 Life
3. A Milli
4. Work featuring Drake
6. Bop
8. Savage

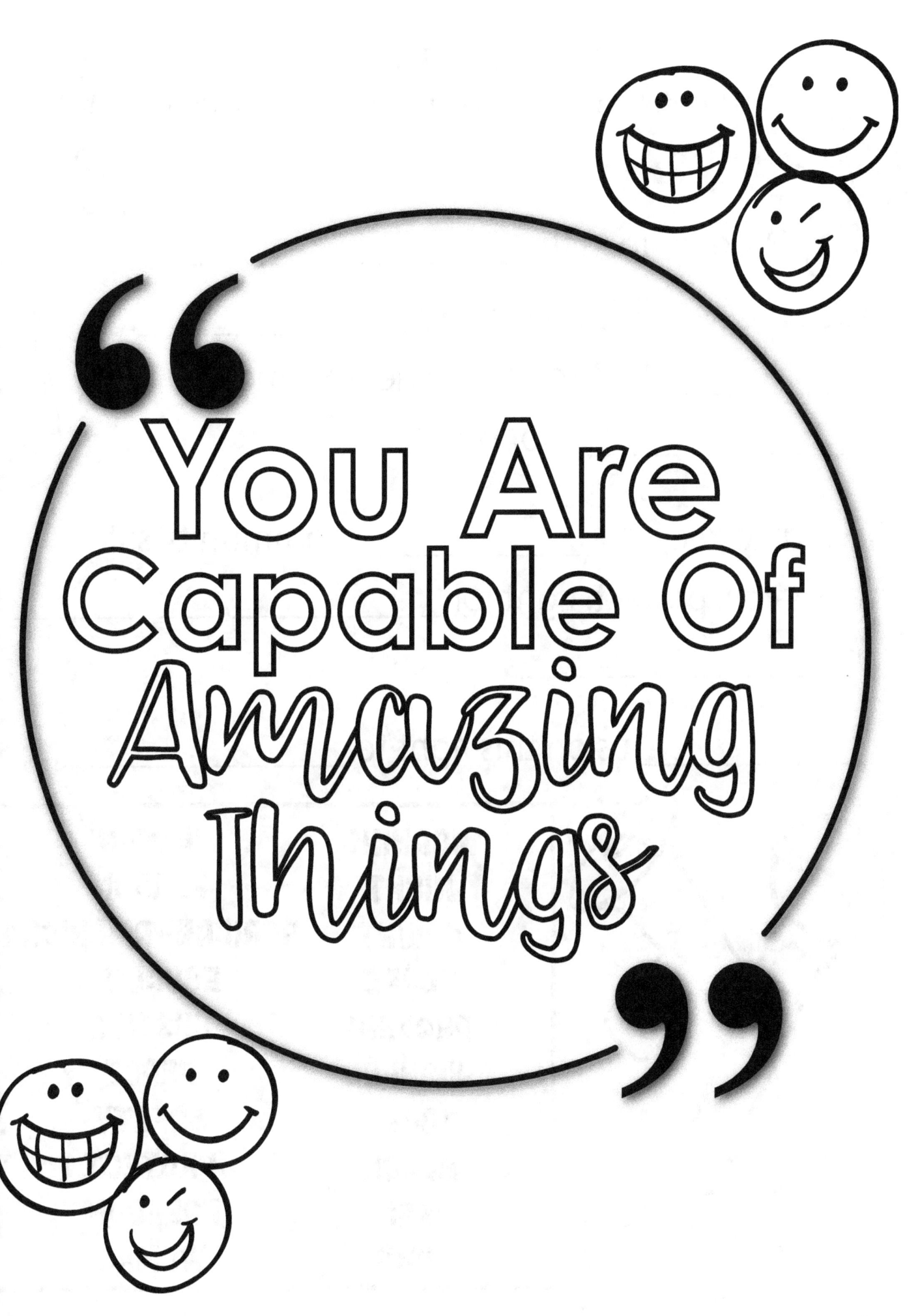

Rap That
Fill in the blanks with words to complete the rap lyric.

Waking up in the _____.
I see the headlines creating a _____.
_____ that this headline isn't another
_____ shot on site.

Trying to keep the _____ community safe.
We march, protect, fight for _____, _____
and _____.

_____ us on this fight to _____.

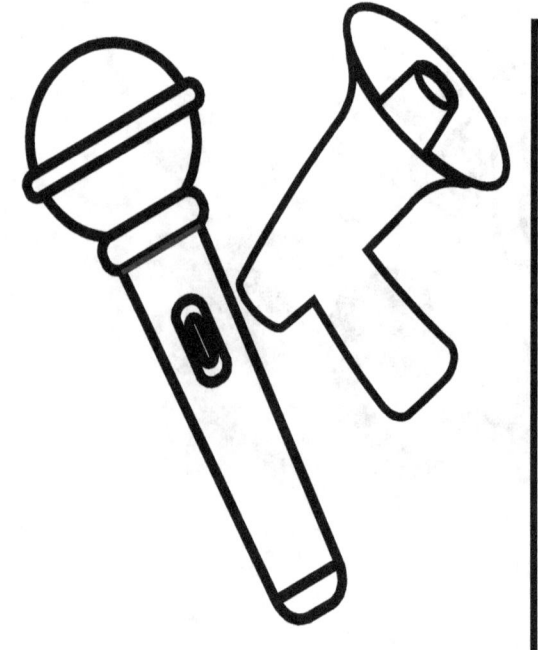

MORNING	HUMAN
NIGHT	PERSON
FRIGHT	AFRICAN-AMERICAN
SCARE	EQUALITY
PRAYING	JUSTICE
WISHFUL	PEACE
YOUNG	SAFETY
BLACK	PROTECT
MAN	FREEDOM
JOIN	WOMAN

Love and Peace Word Search

Find the words that are listed below.

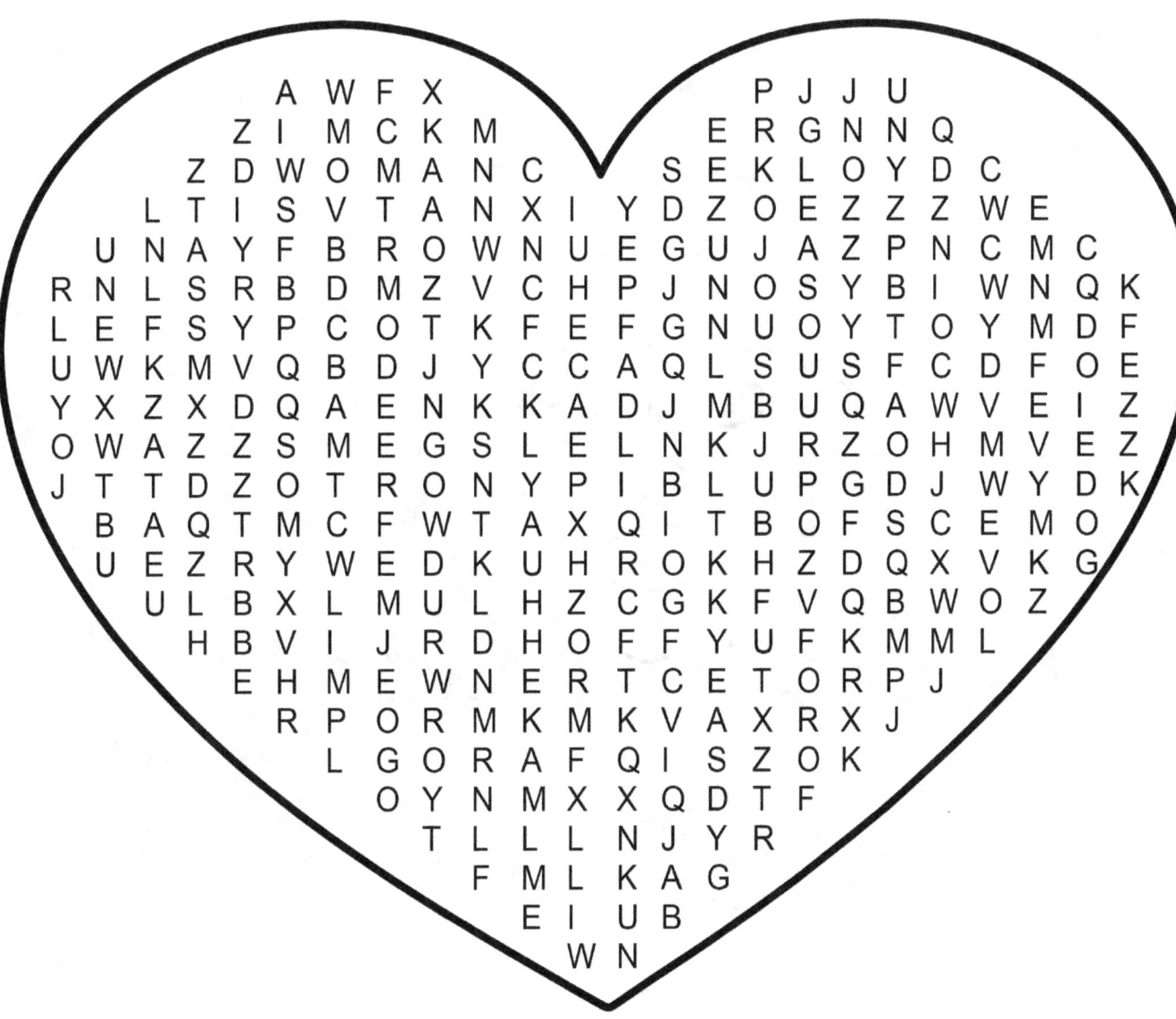

LOVE   BROWN   JUSTICE   FREEDOM   MAN
BLACK   PEACE   PROTECT   CHANGE   WOMAN

Connect The Dots
Complete the drawing by connecting the dots.

Maze Escape
Help Ashley meet up with her friend, Katrina.

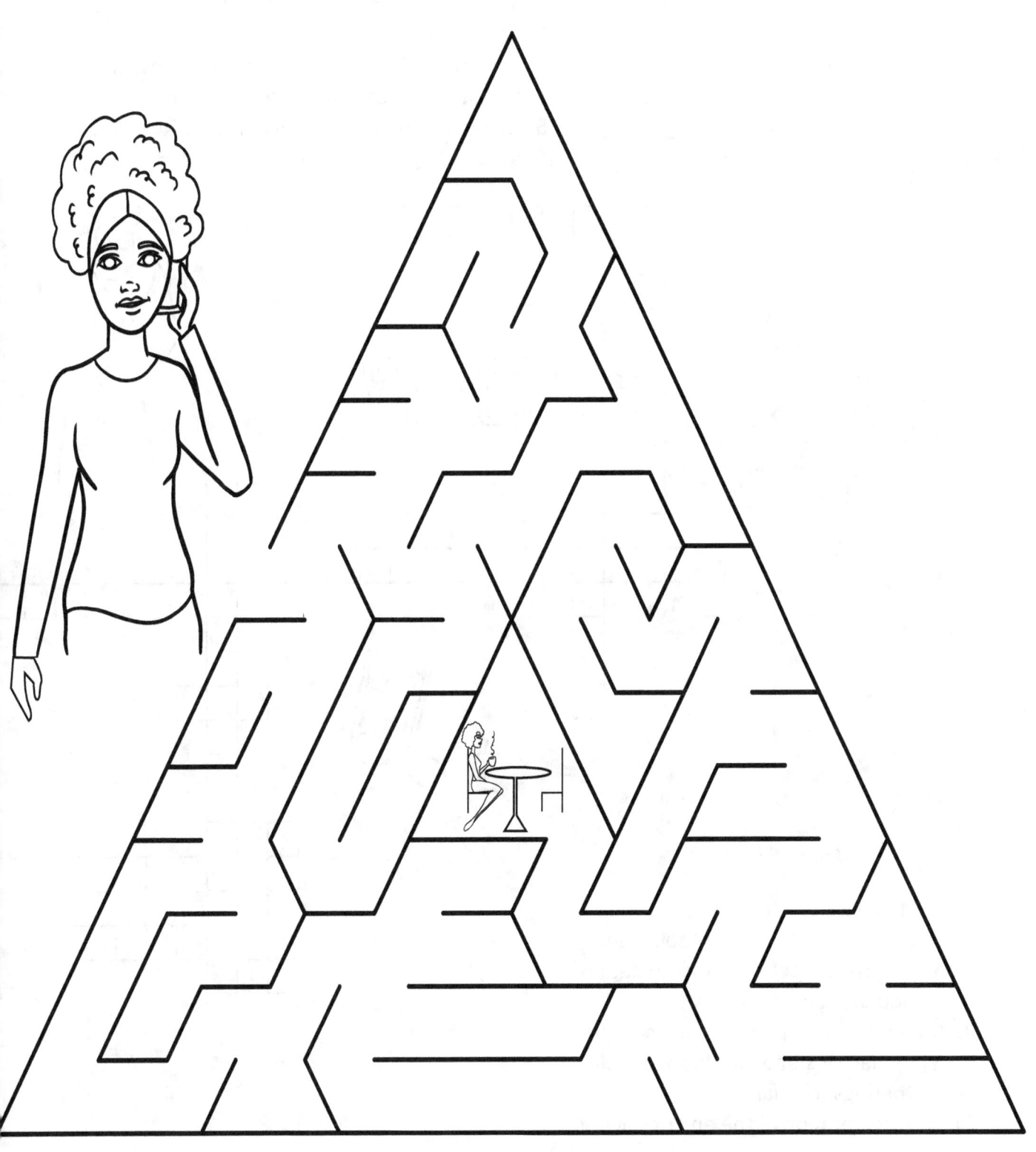

Black Culture

Fill in the crossword with popular elements of black culture

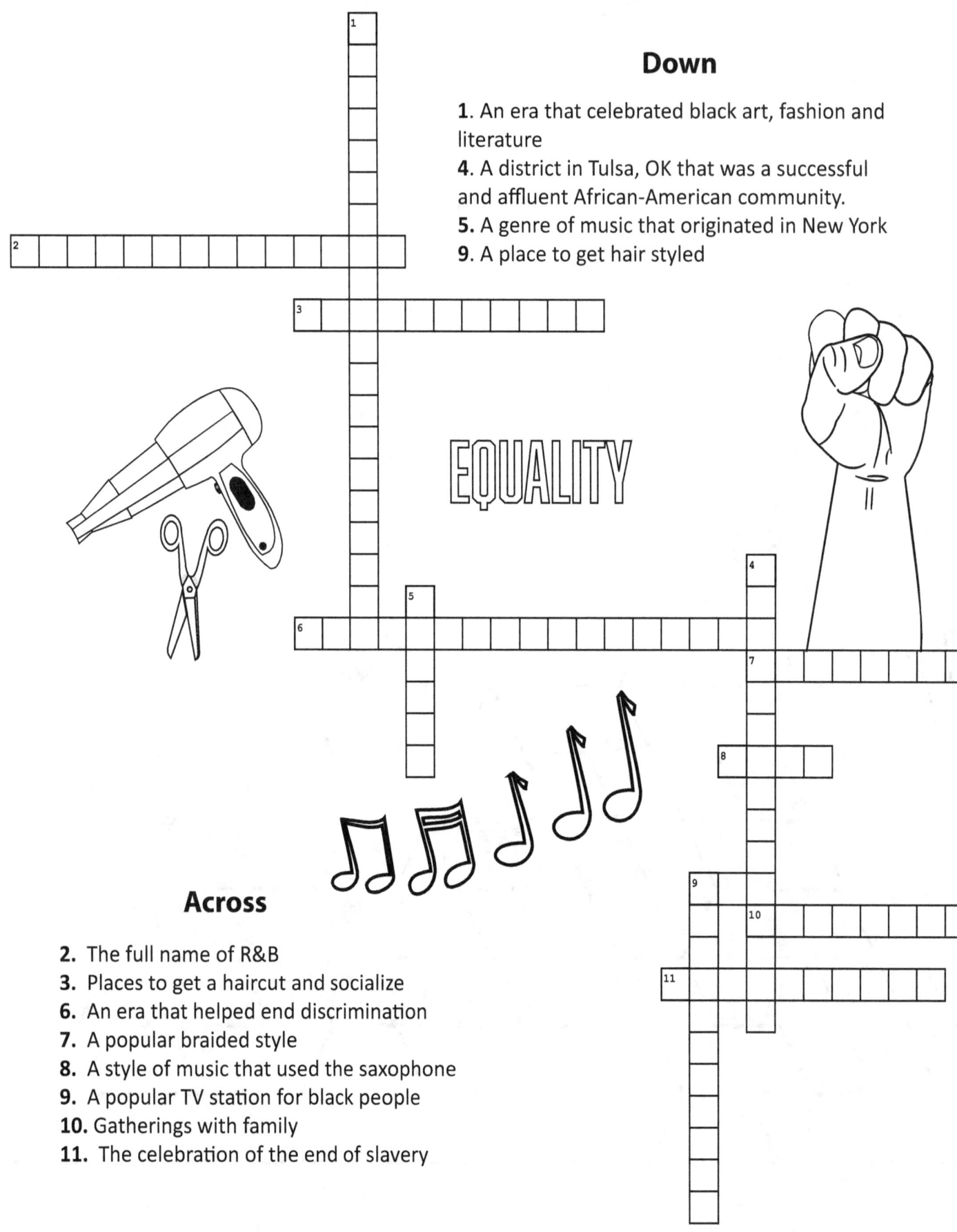

Down

1. An era that celebrated black art, fashion and literature
4. A district in Tulsa, OK that was a successful and affluent African-American community.
5. A genre of music that originated in New York
9. A place to get hair styled

Across

2. The full name of R&B
3. Places to get a haircut and socialize
6. An era that helped end discrimination
7. A popular braided style
8. A style of music that used the saxophone
9. A popular TV station for black people
10. Gatherings with family
11. The celebration of the end of slavery

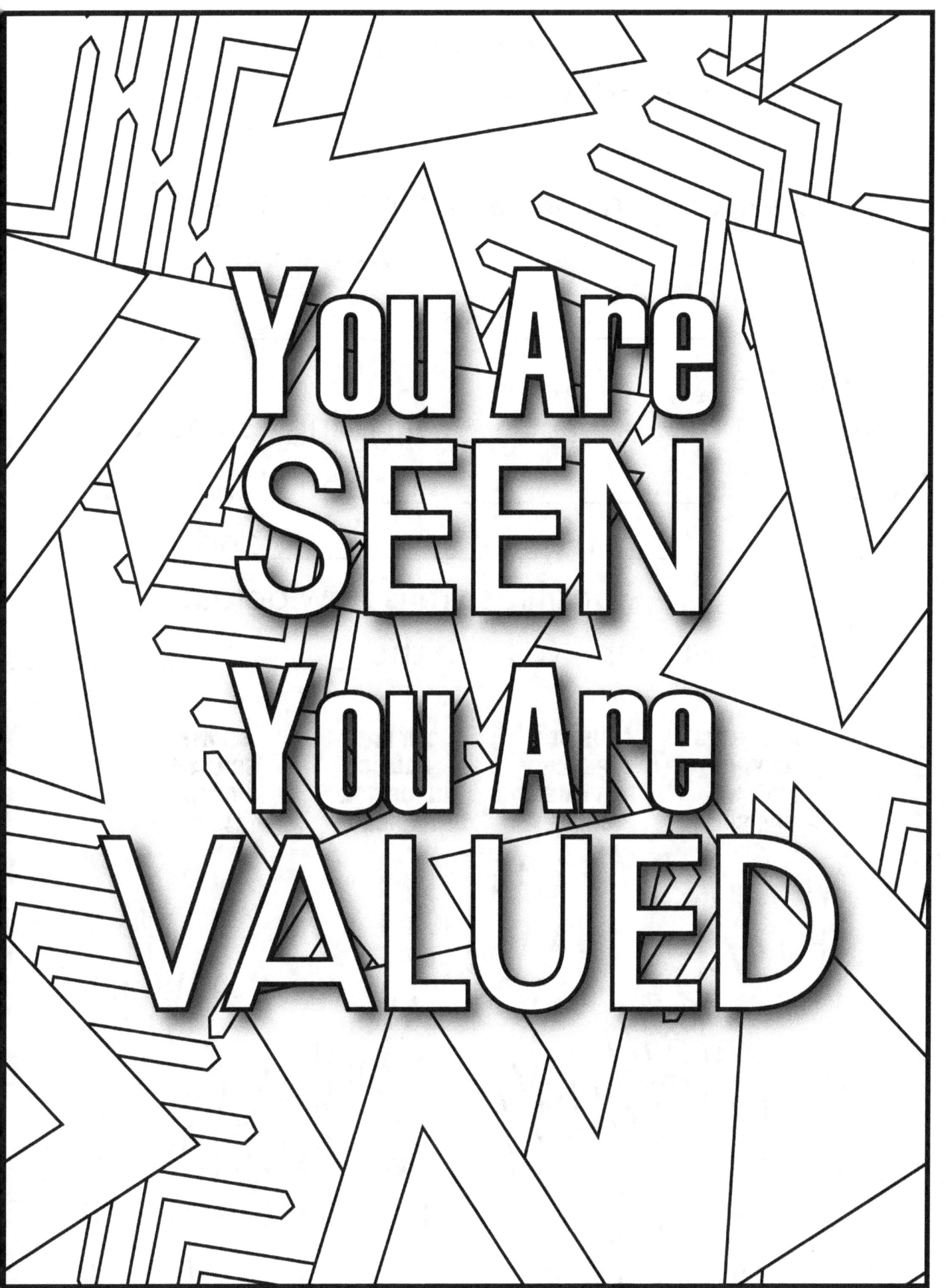

Feel That
Fill in the blanks with words to complete the poem.

Hands up don't shoot, I can't breathe.
We march _____ "Black Lives Matter"
until _____ and _____
is complete.
Supporting the _____ will bring us change.
Exposing the _____ and eliminating the
_____. We _____ and
_____ until racism is now defeated.
Because we will win, we have the _____.

SCREAMING	JUSTICE	THREAT	CHANT
CRYING	PEACE	POLICE	SCREAM
YELLING	MOVEMENT	INJUSTICE	VICTORY
RACISM	CAUSE	MARCH	PAINT

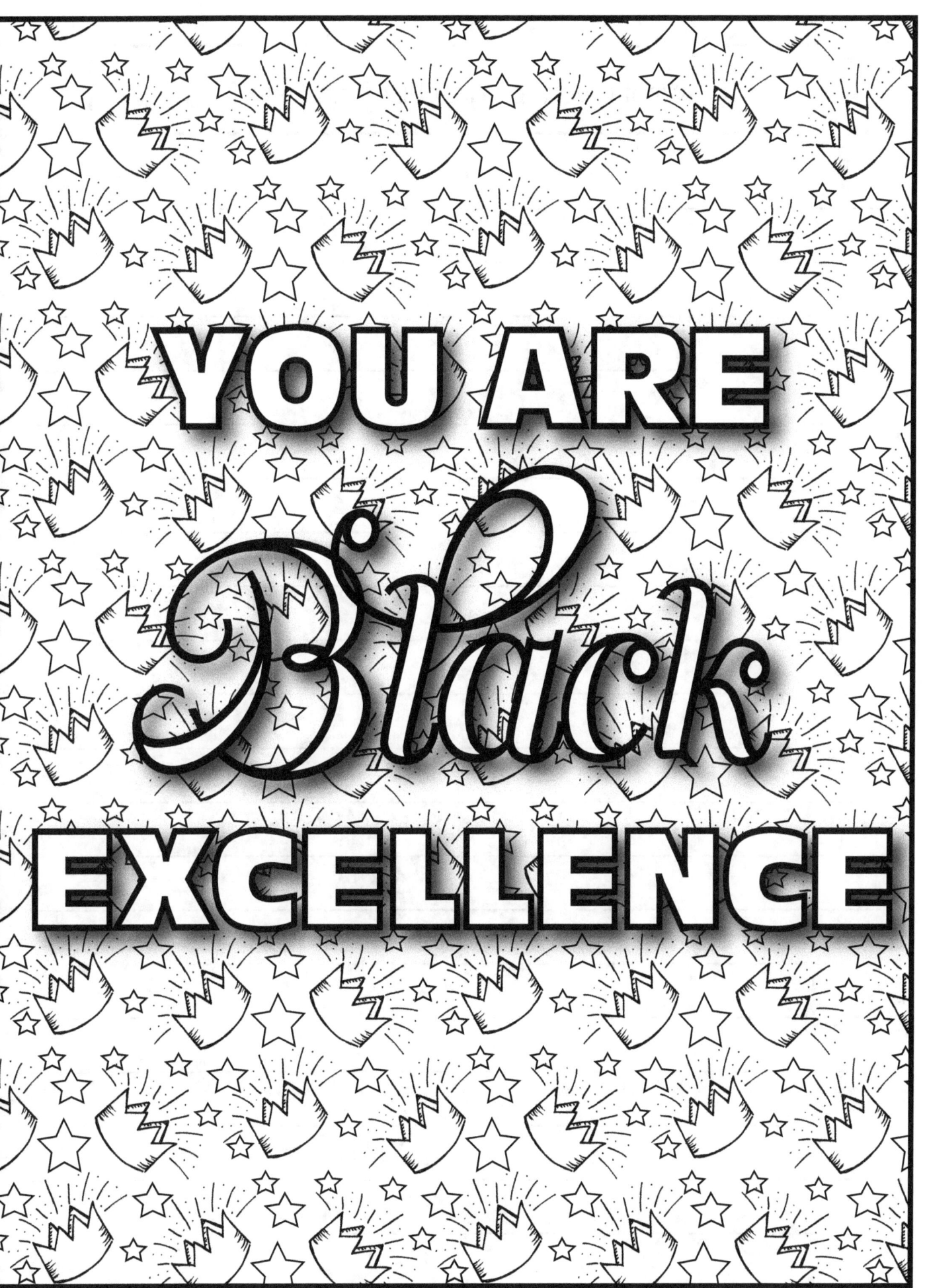

What is your biggest FEAR and why?

How has FEAR held you back from living the life you want?

What is one GOAL you want to accomplish this year? How will you get there?

What is one of your biggest DREAMS?

Name at least three things you can do to ACCOMPLISH your dream.

Answer Key

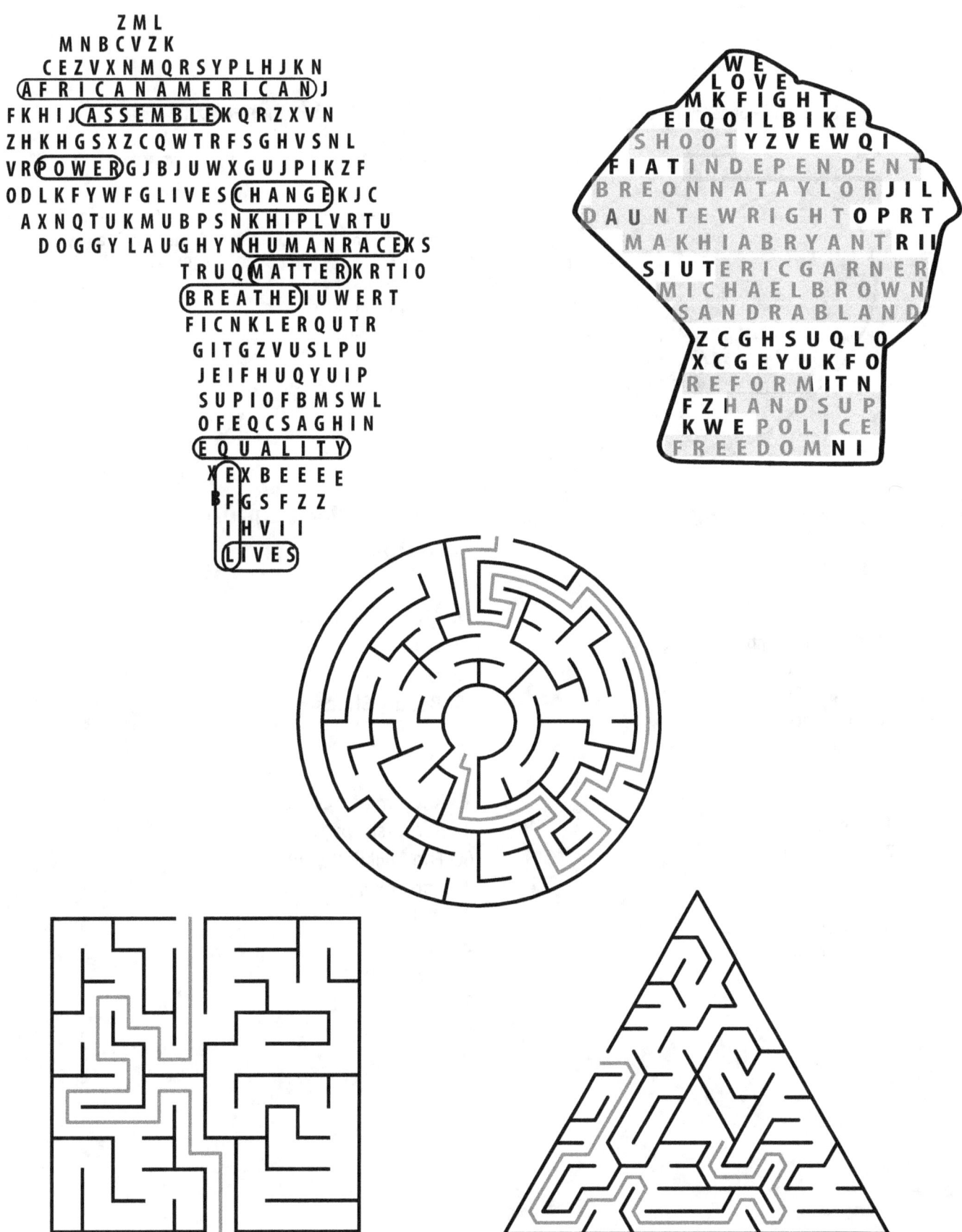

Answer Key

Love and Peace Wordsearch

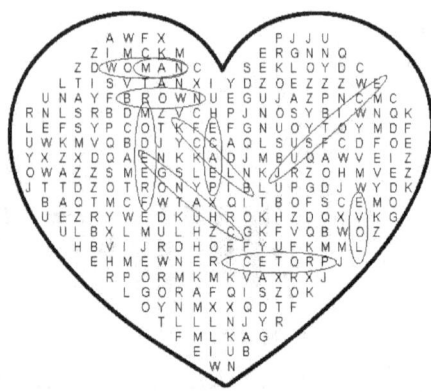

Black TV Shows and Movies

Across
5. Soul
6. Static Shock
7. Black Panther
8. Girlfriends
9. Hidden Figures
10. Princess and The Frog
11. Black Lightning
12. Friday

Down
1. Django
2. The Boondocks
3. The Proud Family
4. Blackish

Black Artists and Music

Across
5. Jay Z
7. Childish Gambino
9. Kanye West
10. Travis Scott
11. Beyonce
12. 50 Cent

Down
1. Kendrick Lamar
2. Nicki Minaj
3. Lil Wayne
4. Rihanna
6. Dababy
8. Meg Thee Stallion

Black Culture

Down
1. The Harlem Renaissance
4. Black Wallstreet
5. Hip Hop
9. Beauty Shops

Across
2. Rhythm and Blues
3. Barbershops
6. The Civil Rights Era
7. Cornrows
8. Jazz
9. BET
10. Reunions
11. Juneteenth